**The Beginning Pianist**

10 beginner piano pieces with teacher duets

D1826693

# Keep in Time 1
## by SHEILA SANDYS-WUNSCH

### Illustrations by Bill Kimber

## Contents

ISBN 0-88797-676-X

FREDERICK HARRIS MUSIC

# Teacher's Notes

This collection of familiar folk tunes is designed for first year players. The hand position remains constant throughout each song. Students can practice finding the hand position before they play. After doing this successfully a number of times, have them do it with their eyes shut (one hand at a time).

Sharps and flats are introduced in some pieces to develop familiarity with the keyboard.

Words are included for all the songs. Have students sing the song before playing it to increase their enjoyment and fluency. Playing and singing together develops sight reading and rhythm skills.

Playing familiar repertoire with someone else is fun and helps students to *Keep in Time!*

*Down in the Valley* is an American folk song with a rhythmic teacher duet.

*Pierrot* includes words in both English and French.

Students are encouraged to sing the verse of *En roulant ma boule* while the teacher plays, joining in the duet by playing the chorus.

*The Cuckoo*, a traditional German song, is written in E major. In the solo part accidentals are used instead of a key signature for ease of reading. The cheerful "cuckoo" of the teacher duet brings this bird to life!

The chorus of the Irish jig *Hi! Ho! The Rattlin' Bog* is presented as a solo. It may also be performed with the student singing the verses while the teacher plays, joining in on the chorus. Have fun keeping track of the verses!

*Lightly Row* introduces B flat and ends with two measures of simple hands together playing.

Students will have fun lifting their hands off the keyboard and clapping in *Love Somebody.*

*Land of the Silver Birch* is a calm reflection on a beautiful Canadian landscape.

The student is encouraged to tap the rhythm of the teacher duet in *My Paddle's Keen and Bright.* The syncopation of the student's solo, captures the energy of the canoe paddle dipping in and out of glistening water.

*J'ai du bon tabac* uses a repeat sign in the middle of the piece to accommodate the words.

4

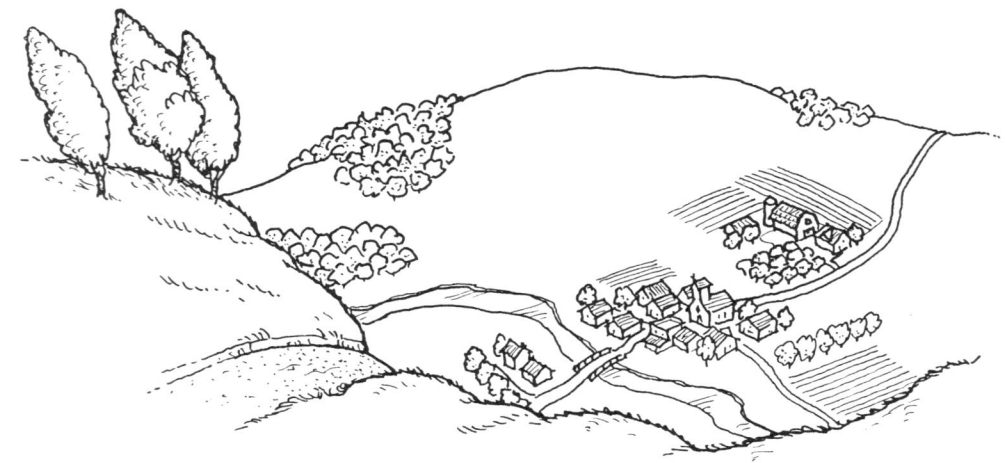

# Down in the Valley

Optional teacher duet
Student plays one octave higher.

Traditional American
arr. Sheila Sandys-Wunsch

Gracioso ♩ = 90

0-88797-676-X/04

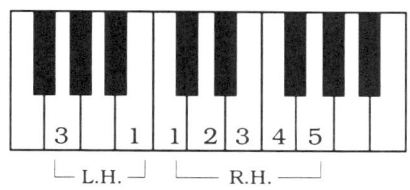

# Down in the Valley

Traditional American
arr. Sheila Sandys-Wunsch

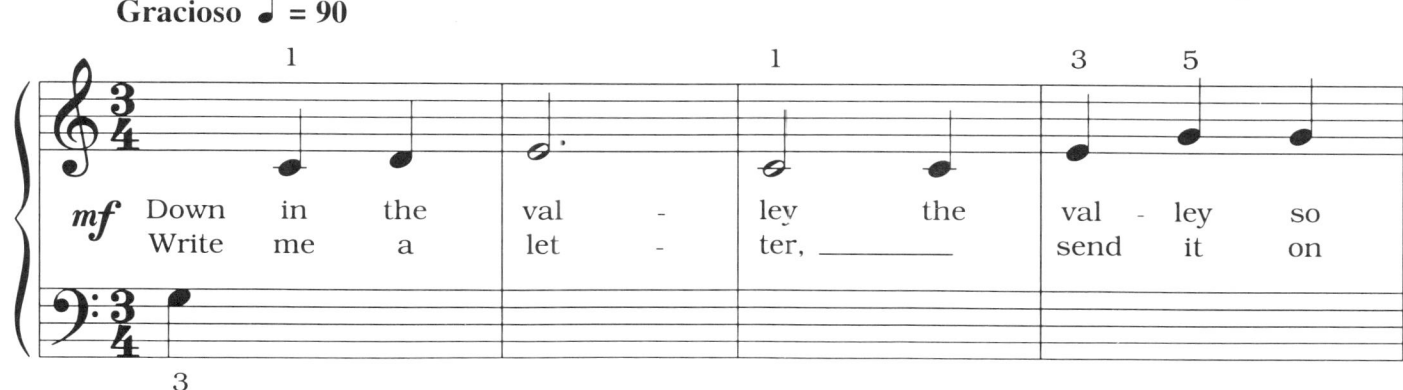

*Grazioso* ♩ = 90

*mf*

Down    in    the    val -    ley    the    val - ley    so
Write    me    a    let -    ter,      send    it    on

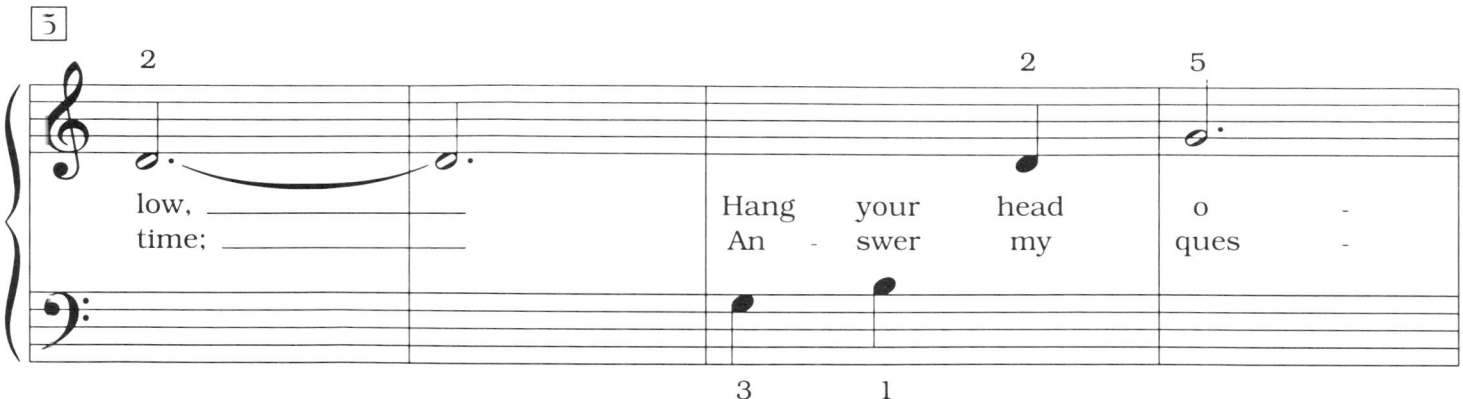

low,         Hang    your    head    o -
time;        An - swer    my    ques -

ver,    hear    the    wind    blow.
tion:    will    you    be    mine?

0-88797-676-X/05

# Pierrot

Optional teacher duet
Student plays one octave higher.

Traditional French
arr. Sheila Sandys-Wunsch

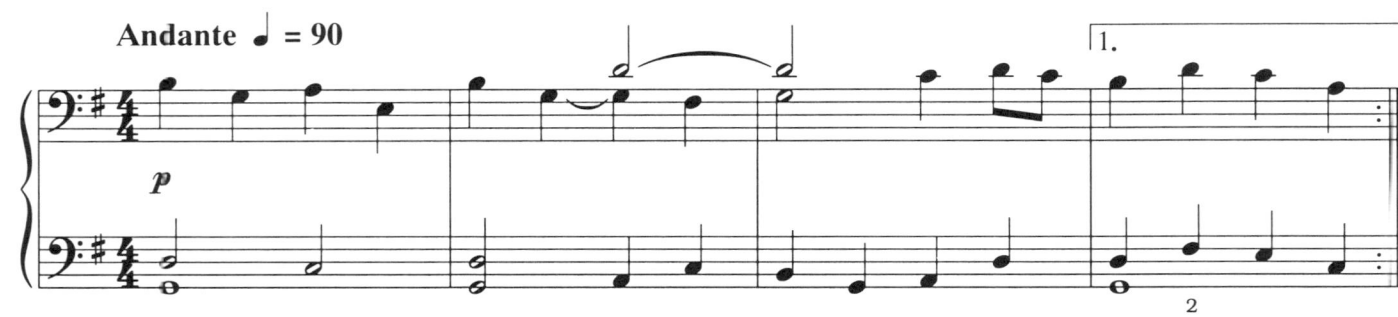

Good Pierrot, be friendly in the clear moonlight,
Your pen will you lend me so that I may write.
I have no more candle, no more flame have I;
Unlock the door handle in God's name I cry.

0-88797-676-X/06

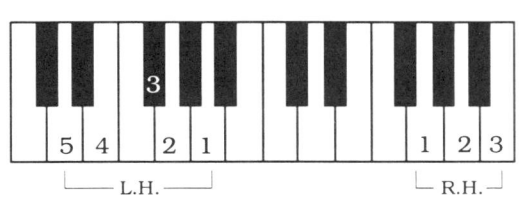

# Pierrot

Traditional French
arr. Sheila Sandys-Wunsch

Andante ♩ = 90

*mp*
Au clair de la lu — ne mon am — i Pier — rot,
Prê — te — moi ta plu — me pour éc — rire un mot.

*mf* Ma chan — delle est mor — te, je n'ai plus de feu;

*mp* Ouv — re moi ta por — te pour l'a — mour de Dieu.

0-88797-676-X/07

8

# En roulant ma boule

Optional teacher duet
Student plays one octave higher.

Traditional French-Canadian
arr. Sheila Sandys-Wunsch

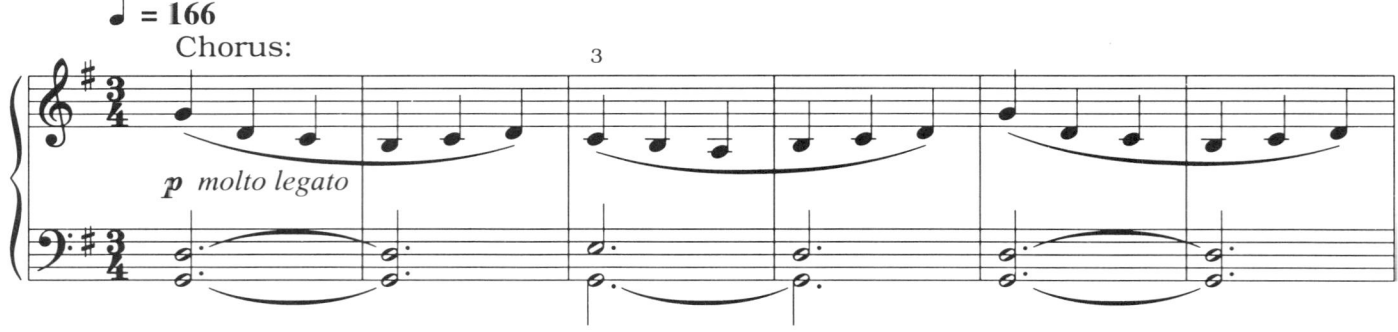

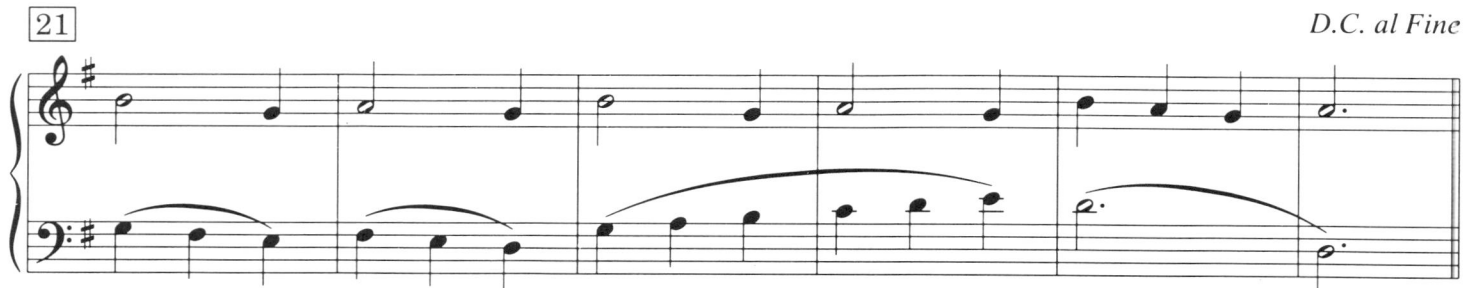

Suggestions for playing the whole song: Play the chorus / Sing the verse / Repeat the chorus.

Chorus:

Keep the ball a-rolling away,
Keep the ball a-rolling.
Keep the ball a-rolling away,
Keep the ball a-rolling.

Verse:

Behind our house there is a pond,
Keep the ball a-rolling.
Three fine fat ducks swim all around,
Keep the ball a-rolling.
Three fine fat ducks swim all around,
Away, away, keep rolling away.

0-88797-676-X/03

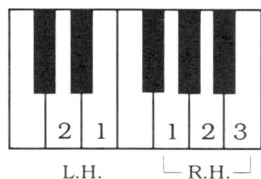

# En roulant ma boule

♩ = 166

Chorus:

Traditional French-Canadian
arr. Sheila Sandys-Wunsch

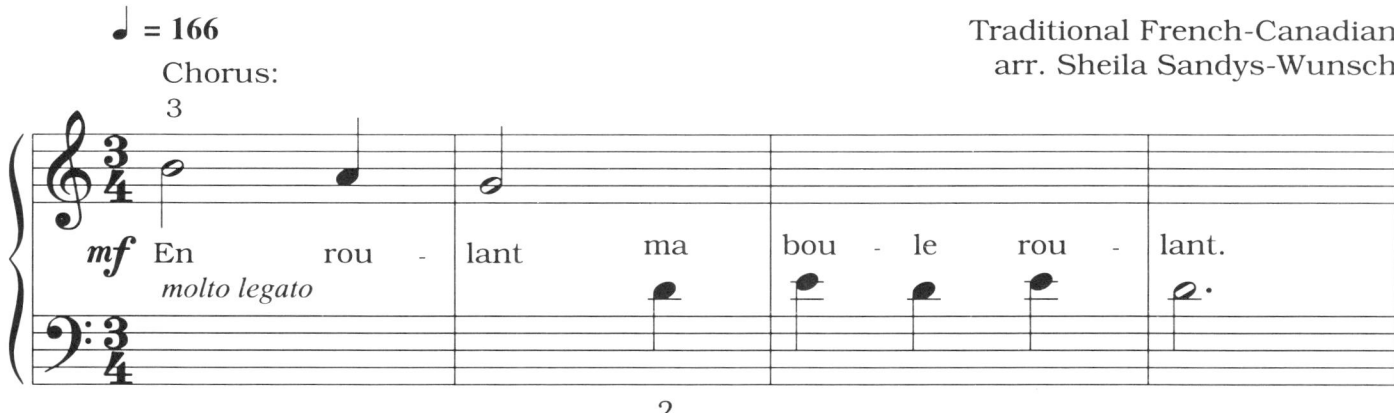

En rou - lant ma bou - le rou - lant.

*molto legato*

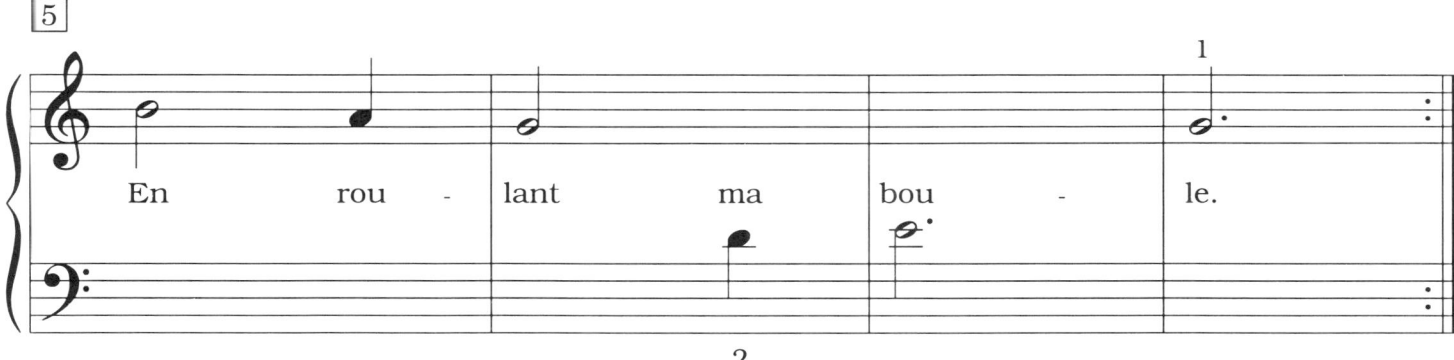

En rou - lant ma bou - le.

Suggestions for playing the whole song: Play the chorus / Sing the verse / Repeat the chorus.

Chorus:

En roulant ma boule roulant.
En roulant ma boule.
En roulant ma boule roulant.
En roulant ma boule.

Verse:

Derrière chez nous y'a un étang,
en roulant ma boule.
Trois beaux canards s'en vont baignant,
en roulant ma boule.
Trois beaux canards s'en vont baignant,
Rouli, roulant ma boule roulant.

When you know this song well, play it on the black keys using this fingering:

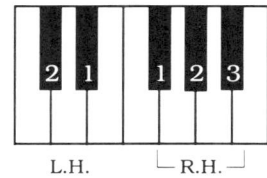

0-88797-676-X/09

# The Cuckoo

Optional teacher duet
Student plays one octave higher.

Traditional German
arr. Sheila Sandys-Wunsch

Lightly ♩ = 120

0-88797-676-X/10

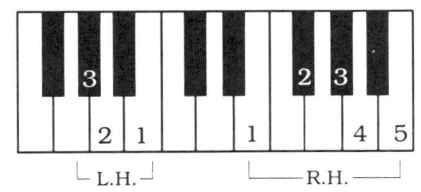

# The Cuckoo

Traditional German
arr. Sheila Sandys-Wunsch

**Lightly** ♩ = 120

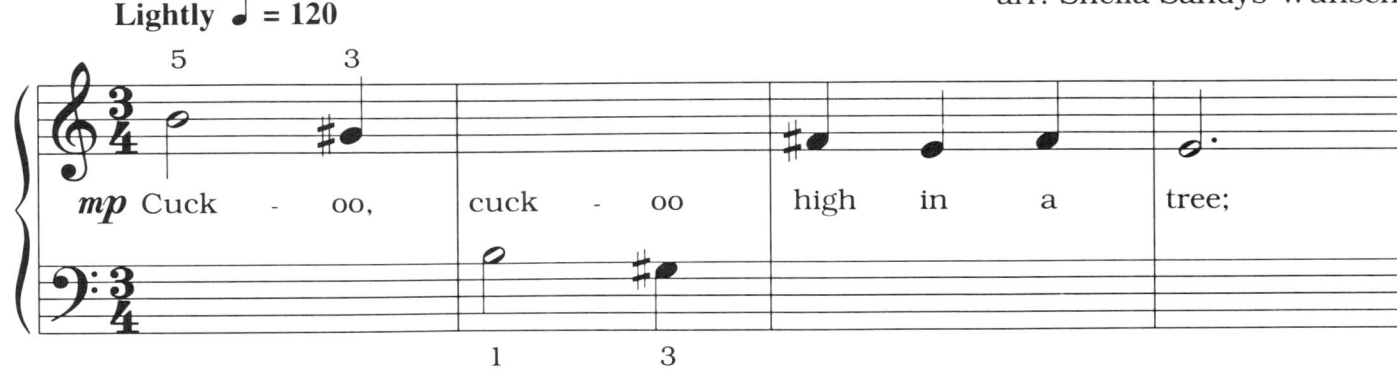

*mp* Cuck - oo, cuck - oo high in a tree;

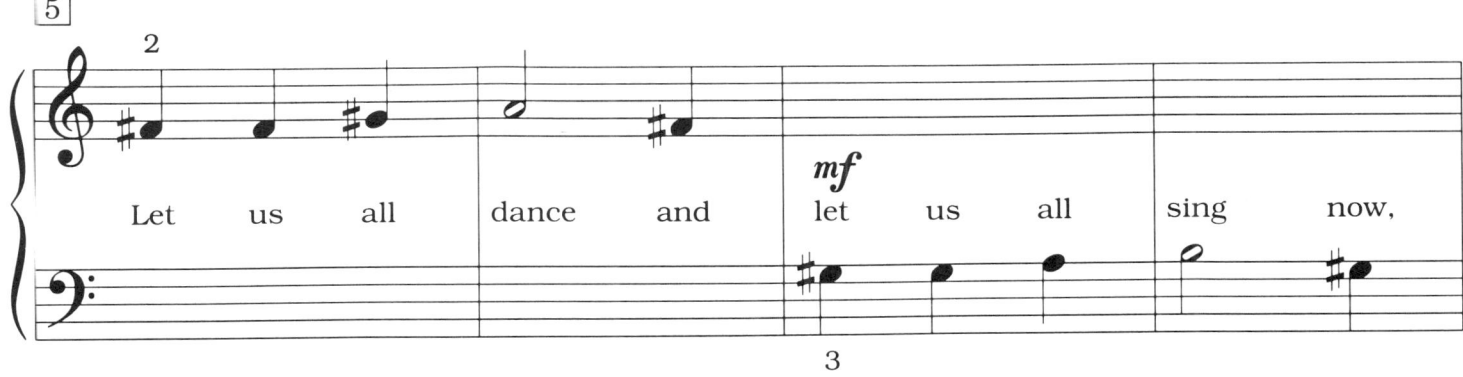

Let us all dance and *mf* let us all sing now,

Spring - time, spring - time, soon it will be.
*mp*

0-88797-676-X/11

# Hi! Ho! The Rattlin' Bog

Optional teacher duet
Student plays one octave higher.

Traditional Irish
arr. Sheila Sandys-Wunsch

**With spirit** ♩ = 132

Chorus:

*Fine*

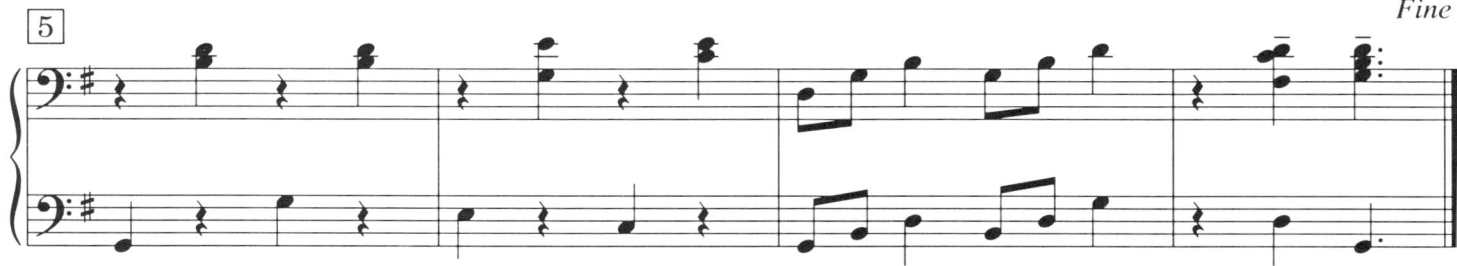

Verse: 9

*D.C. al Fine*

Suggestions for playing the whole song: Play the chorus / Sing the verse / Play the chorus / Sing the verse / End with the chorus.

Chorus:

Hi! Ho! The rattlin' bog,
the bog down in the valley-O,
Hi! Ho! The rattlin' bog,
the bog down in the valley-O.

Verse:

1. Now in this bog there is a tree,
   a rare tree, a rattlin' tree:
   The tree in the bog,
   and the bog down in the valley-O.

2. Now on this tree there is a limb,
   a rare limb, a rattlin' limb:
   The limb on the tree
   and the tree in the bog
   And the bog down in the valley-O.

With each new verse add an element: branch, nest, egg, etc.

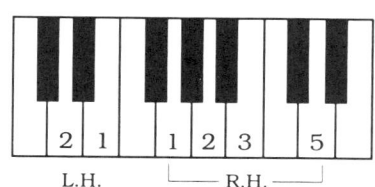

L.H.    R.H.

# Hi! Ho! The Rattlin' Bog

**With spirit** ♩ = 132

Chorus:

Traditional Irish
arr. Sheila Sandys-Wunsch

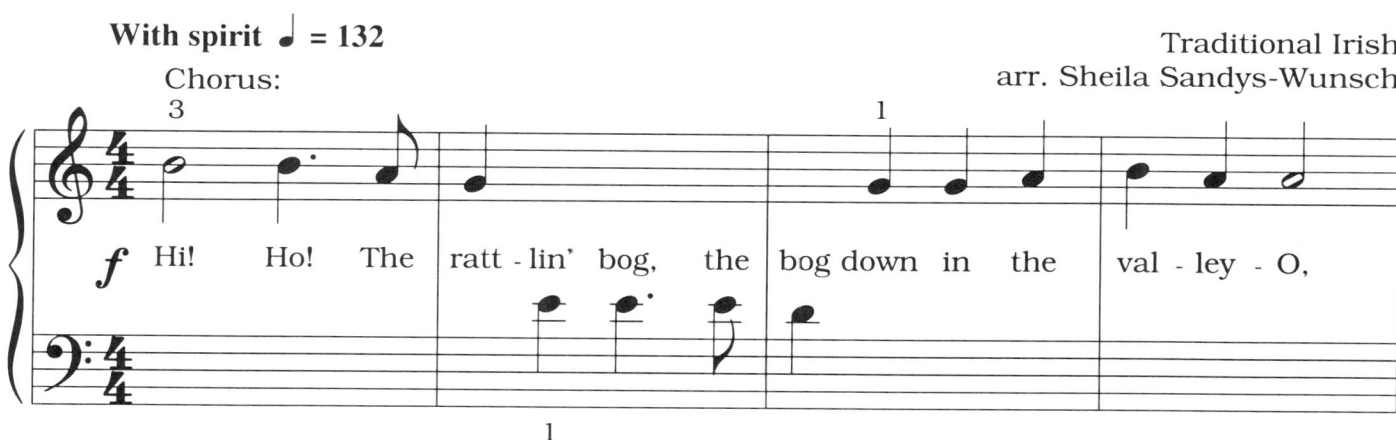

Hi! Ho! The ratt-lin' bog, the bog down in the val-ley-O,

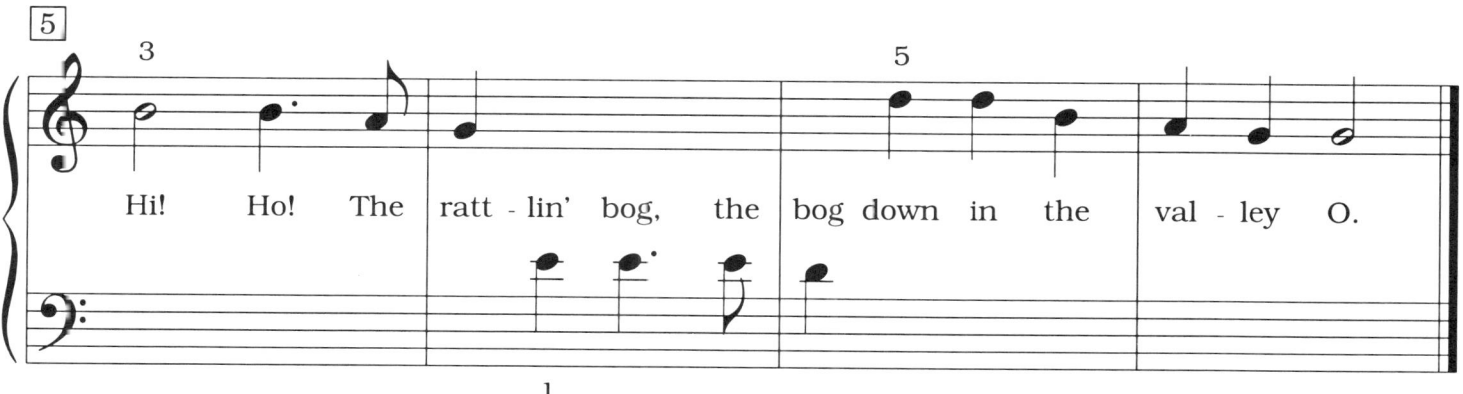

Hi! Ho! The ratt-lin' bog, the bog down in the val-ley O.

When you know this song well, play it on the black keys using this fingering:

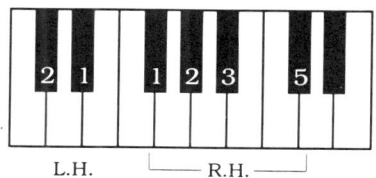

L.H.    R.H.

0-88797-676-X/13

# Lightly Row

Optional teacher duet
Student plays one octave higher.

Traditional German
arr. Sheila Sandys-Wunsch

**Brightly** ♩ = 116

*mp*

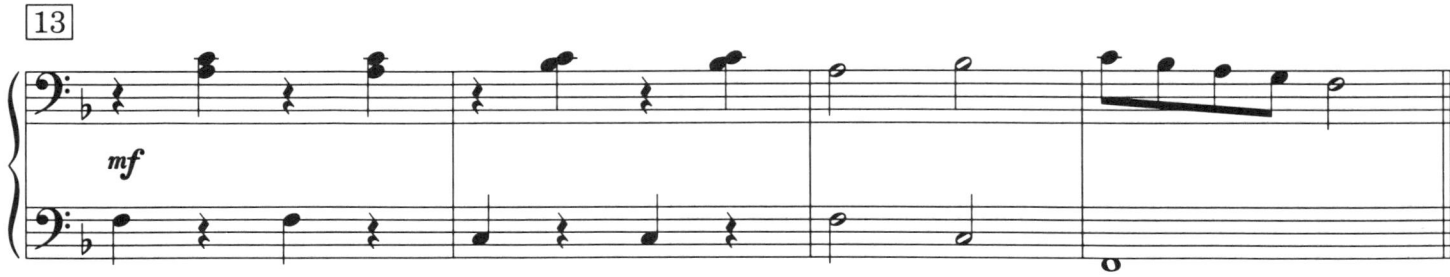

*mf*

0-88797-676-X/14

2
4
5 4 3 1
1 2 3 5
L.H.
R.H.

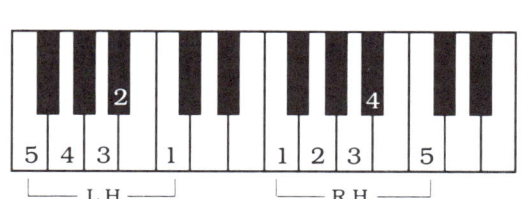

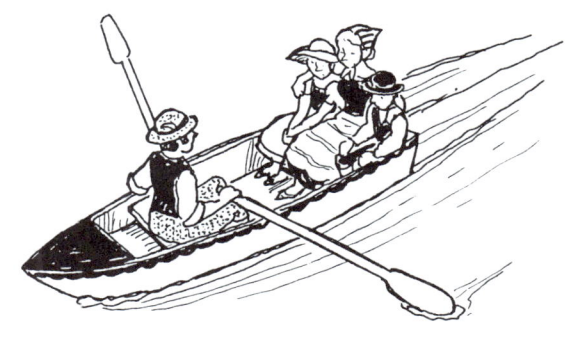

# Lightly Row

Traditional German
arr. Sheila Sandys-Wunsch

**Brightly** ♩ = 116

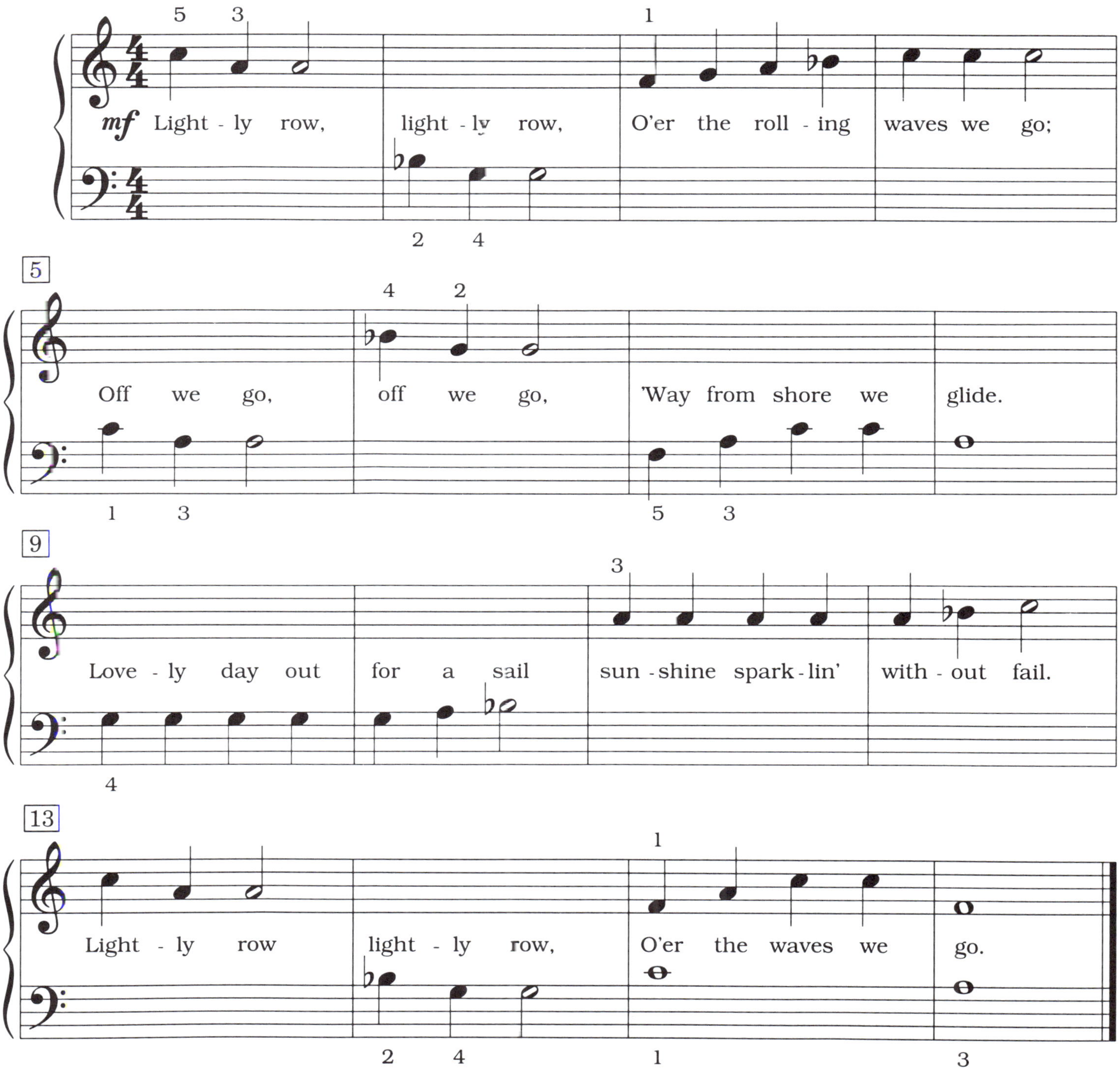

mf
Light - ly row, light - ly row, O'er the roll - ing waves we go;
Off we go, off we go, 'Way from shore we glide.
Love - ly day out for a sail sun - shine spark - lin' with - out fail.
Light - ly row light - ly row, O'er the waves we go.
5
9
13

# Love Somebody

Optional teacher duet
Student plays one octave higher.

Traditional American
arr. Sheila Sandys-Wunsch

**Brightly** ♩ = 144

Love somebody, yes I do! Love somebody, yes I do!
Love somebody, yes I do! Love somebody but I won't tell who!

0-88797-676-X/16

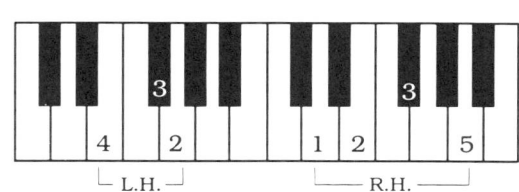

# Love Somebody

Traditional American
arr. Sheila Sandys-Wunsch

**Brightly** ♩ = 144

*mf*

♩ = clap

0-88797-676-X/17

# Land of the Silver Birch

Optional teacher duet
Student plays one octave higher.

Traditional Canadian
arr. Sheila Sandys-Wunsch

Calmly ♩ = 104

0-88797-676-X/18

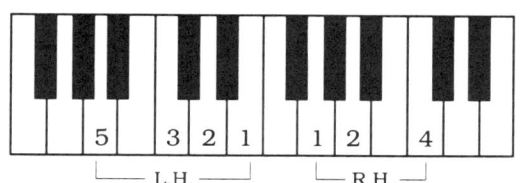

# Land of the Silver Birch

Traditional Canadian
arr. Sheila Sandys-Wunsch

**Calmly** ♩ = 104

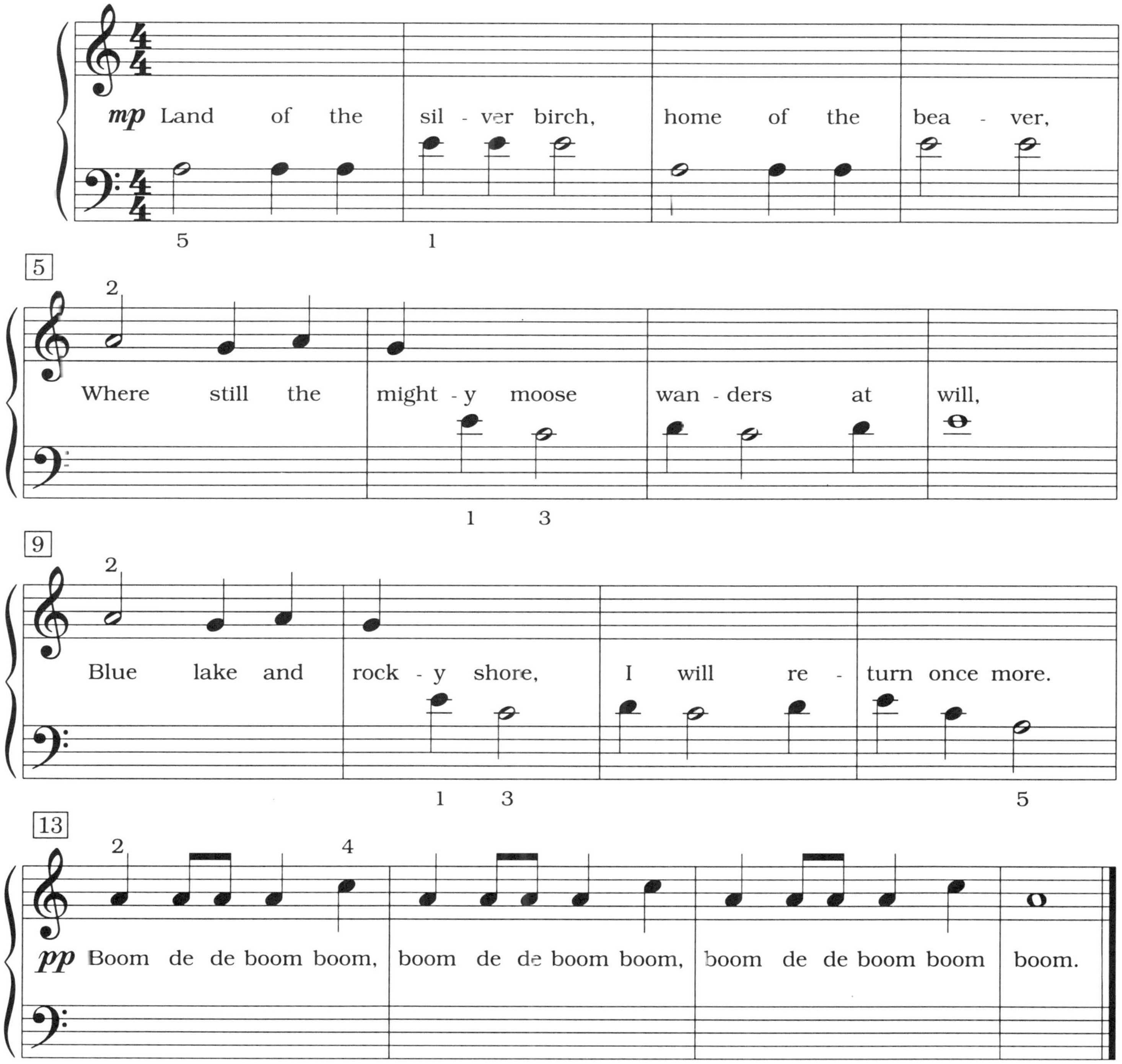

*mp* Land of the sil - ver birch, home of the bea - ver,

Where still the might - y moose wan - ders at will,

Blue lake and rock - y shore, I will re - turn once more.

*pp* Boom de de boom boom, boom de de boom boom, boom de de boom boom boom.

0-88797-676-X/19

# My Paddle's Keen and Bright

Optional teacher duet
Student plays one octave higher.

Traditional Canadian
arr. Sheila Sandys-Wunsch

Suggestions for playing the whole song:

1.  The student plays the melody with the teacher accompanying (mm. 1-8).
    The teacher plays the melody (mm. 9-16) while the student taps the following
    rhythmic pattern on the wood of the piano:
    The student plays the melody with the teacher accompanying (mm. 1-8).

2.  The student plays the melody with the teacher accompanying (mm. 1-8).
    The teacher plays the melody (mm. 9-16) while the student sings verse 1.
    The student plays the melody with the teacher accompanying (mm. 1-8).
    The teacher plays the melody (mm. 9-16) while the student sings verse 2.
    The student plays the melody with the teacher accompanying (mm. 1-8).

0-88797-676-X/20

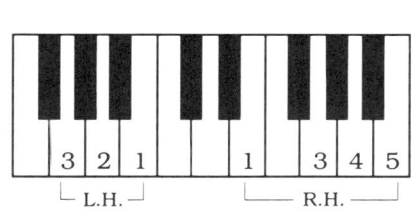

# My Paddle's Keen and Bright

Traditional Canadian
arr. Sheila Sandys-Wunsch

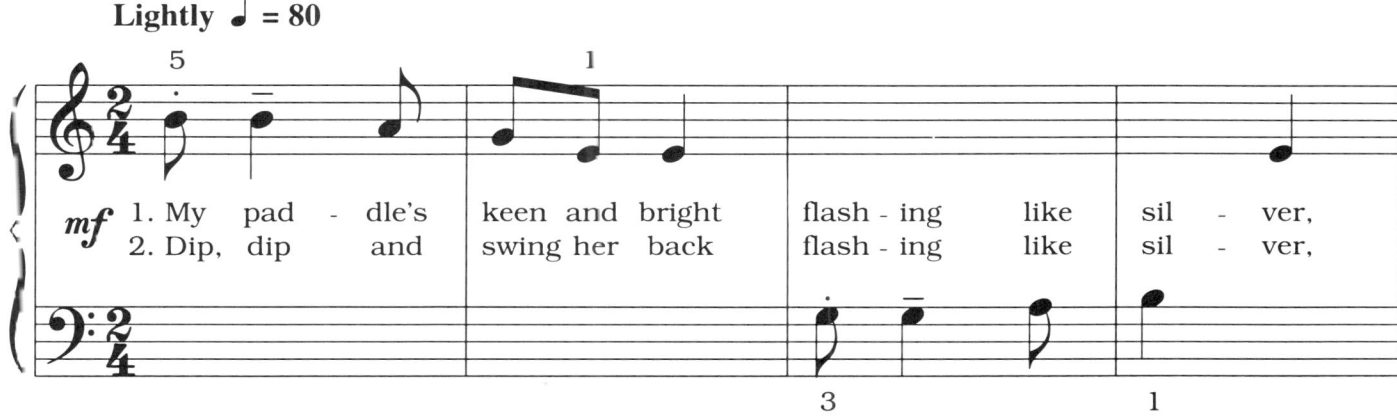

0-88797-676-X/21

# J'ai du bon tabac

Optional teacher duet
Student plays one octave higher.

Traditional French
arr. Sheila Sandys-Wunsch

Briskly ♩ = 116

In my little snuff-box I've such good snuff, Sir,
very fine snuff, but there's none for you.
I have the best, as you may suppose,
but there is none for your poor old nose.
In my little snuff-box I've such good snuff, Sir,
very fine snuff, but there's none for you.

0-88797-676-X/22

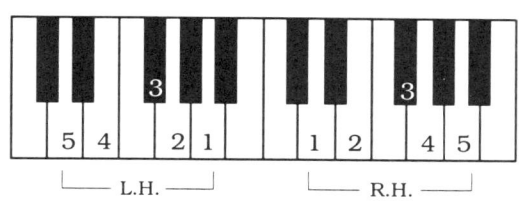

# J'ai du bon tabac

Traditional French
arr. Sheila Sandys-Wunsch

**Briskly** ♩ = 116

0-88797-676-X/23